Friendship Or Flirtationship

Zabed Mohammad, PhD.

EDUCATOR & RESEARCHER
CANADA

EDITED BY

DR. K. W. CHRISTOPHERSON
PHD, MED, BED, BA.

Kids Edu Care

Library of Congress Cataloging-in-Publication Data
ISBN: 978-1-998923-24-3

Publisher
Kids Edu Care Inc.
Children's Dedicated Learning Series
Website: www.kidseducare.ca
Illustration Copyright © 2023 by
Kids Edu Care Inc.
Canada

Illustration & Design
Bee Digital

beedigital.asia

info@beedigital.asia

Friendship and Flirtationship

Friendships are bonds between two or more people who want to engage with one another because of mutual interest in each other's thoughts, feelings, and experiences. Friendships work on reciprocal trust, respect, and emotional support.

A flirtationship, in contrast, is when people flirt with the hope of it leading to romance, dating, or a relationship. It can involve friendship, but extends further with the possibility that it leads to something more. There are two types of flirtatious behaviour that people can engage in. The first is when two people engage in flirtatious behaviour without expecting anything more. They just flirt. The second is when one of the individuals involved engages in flirtatious behaviour hoping that it will lead to a relationship of some kind between the two individuals.

An Unexpected Connection

Sarah and Zakaria,
Sarah and Zakaria have been partnered for a school project. Little did they know that this chance arrangement would lead them on a journey of exploring the dynamics of friendship and flirtation and how they could navigate this relationship to find peace in their lives.

The Blossoming Friendship

Sarah and Zakaria quickly developed a close bond as they spent more time together. They shared common interests, supported each other in their school work, enjoyed each others company, and began to spend more time together. It was during this time that they also began to feel something more than just friendship – the sparks of flirtation were beginning to ignite.

The Flirtatious Temptation

As Sarah and Zakaria's connection grew stronger, they started experiencing flirtatious moments. They found themselves drawn to each other, but also became aware of the potential consequences and conflicts that could arise.

Seeking Guidance in the Holy Quran

Sarah and Zakaria turned to the Holy Quran for guidance. They explored verses on modesty, self-control, and the importance of preserving personal and social harmony as they sought to align their day-to-day discussions and actions with the teaching of Islam. As the Al Quran encourages in Surah Al-Kahf, Allah (SWT) says,

"And keep yourself patient with those who call upon their Lord in the morning and the evening, seeking His countenance. And let not your eyes pass beyond them, desiring adornments of the worldly life..." (18:28).

True friends provide emotional support, share common values, and remind each other of their purpose in life.

Drawing Inspiration from Role Models

Sarah and Zakaria sought inspiration from the life of the Prophet Muhammad (peace be upon him) and their companions. They saw that friendship was built on faith, trust and respect and they acknowledged that mistakes happen. They realized they needed to build their friendship and were willing to forgive each other and seek Allah's mercy, allowing their friendship to grow stronger.

Understanding the Consequences

Sarah and Zakaria delved into the hadiths of the Prophet Muhammad (peace be upon him) that emphasized the consequences of engaging with others. The Prophet Muhammad (SWT) said:

"A good friend and a bad friend are like a perfume-seller and a blacksmith:
The perfume-seller might give you some perfume as a gift, or you might buy some from him, or at least you might smell its fragrance. As for the blacksmith, he might singe your clothes, and at the very least, you will breathe in the fumes of the furnace" (Sahih Al-Bukhari, ##?).

It is important to choose friends who have a positive influence, encourage growth and goodness, and support each other in their faith journey. However, friendships can sometimes lead to emotional turmoil, strained relationships and a loss of spiritual growth. When this happens, it is important to return to faith to seek guidance and support.

Building Strong Foundations

Sarah and Zakaria recognized the importance of building their friendship on a foundation of trust, respect and mutual understanding. They understood that a strong friends would bring them peace and stability in the long run. They believed that positive friendships have a profound effect and influence while negative friendships can lead one astray. Here, the Al Quran warns us in the Surah Al-Furqan:

"And the Day the wrongdoer will bite on his hands [in regret] he will say, 'Oh, I wish I had taken with the Messenger a way. Oh, woe to me! I wish I had not taken that one as a friend. He led me away from the remembrance after it had come to me. And ever

is Satan, to man, a deserter' " (25:27-29).

Communication and Boundaries

Sarah and Zakaria engaged in open and honest communication, discussing their feelings and setting clear boundaries. They recognized that setting limits would protect their friendship and prevent flirtatious behaviour. In the Holy Quran, Allah (SWT) advises us:

"Tell the believing men to reduce [some] of their vision and guard their private parts. That is purer for them. Indeed, Allah is Acquainted with what they do"

(Surah An-Nur, 24:30).

This verse directs people to lower their gaze, meaning to avoid prolonged or inappropriate staring, and to guard their modesty.

Self-Control and Self-Awareness

Sarah and Zakaria realized the importance of self-control and self-awareness. They understood that being mindful of their intentions and actions would help them navigate the challenges of a flirtatious relationship and make choices aligned with their faith.

The Power of Remembrance

Sarah and Zakaria discovered the power of remembrance (dhikr) in their friendship, and incorporated the remembrance of Allah (SWT) in their interactions, seeking His guidance and blessings in strengthening their bond while maintaining their commitment to a peaceful life.
In the Holy Quran, Allah (SWT) says,

"Unquestionably, the allies of Allah – there will be no fear concerning them, nor will they grieve. Those who believed and were fearing Allah"
(Surah Yunus, 10:62-63).

This passage assures believers that the true allies or friends of Allah, those who have faith and fear Him, will have no fear or grief. It emphasizes that having a strong friendship with Allah brings peace, protection, and contentment.

Nurturing Other Relationships

Sarah and Zakaria also acknowledged the importance of maintaining and nurturing their other relationships. They realized that a healthy social life involved spending time with family and friends and engaging in community activities, promoting harmony and peace.

Resisting Peer Pressure

Sarah and Zakaria faced peer pressure from friends who encouraged them to pursue a flirtatious relationship. They remained steadfast in their commitment to their values, however, drawing strength from the teachings of Islam and seeking support from like-minded individuals.

The Blessings of Friendship

Sarah and Zakaria recognized the blessings of their friendship. They appreciated the support, laughter, and comfort they found in each other without crossing the boundaries set by their faith.
In the Holy Quran, Allah (SWT) declares,

"And [yet], among the people are those who take other than Allah as equals [to Him]. They love them as they [should] love Allah. But those who believe are stronger in love for Allah" (Surah Al Baqarah, 2:165).

This verse highlights the contrast between those who prioritize their love and friendship with Allah and those who give equal or greater love to worldly desires or other beings. Believers are encouraged to have a stronger love and devotion for Allah above all else.

Gratitude and Contentment

Sarah and Zakaria practiced gratitude and contentment, understanding that true happiness and peace lie in being grateful for what Allah (SWT) has provided. They cherished their friendship and found contentment in knowing they were making choices aligned with their faith.

Seeking Guidance from Scholars

Sarah and Zakaria sought guidance from knowledgeable scholars who could provide them with a deeper understanding of Islamic teachings. They attended lectures, asked questions, and learned how to navigate their friendship while upholding Islamic values.

Reflecting on Inner Growth

Sarah and Zakaria engaged in self-reflection, assessing their personal growth and spiritual development. They recognized that their friendship should be a source of encouragement, supporting each other's journey towards becoming better individuals.

Respecting Personal and Social Boundaries

Sarah and Zakaria understood the importance of respecting personal and social boundaries. They recognized that crossing these boundaries could lead to strained relationships and disrupt the peace and harmony in their lives.

Empathy and Compassion

Sarah and Zakaria practiced empathy and compassion towards each other and those around them. They understood the impact their actions could have on others, and strived to make choices that would bring joy, peace, and understanding.

Forgiveness and Redemption

Sarah and Zakaria learned the power of forgiveness and redemption. They acknowledged that mistakes might happen along their journey, but they were willing to forgive each other and themselves, seeking guidance from Allah (SWT) and accepting His mercy.

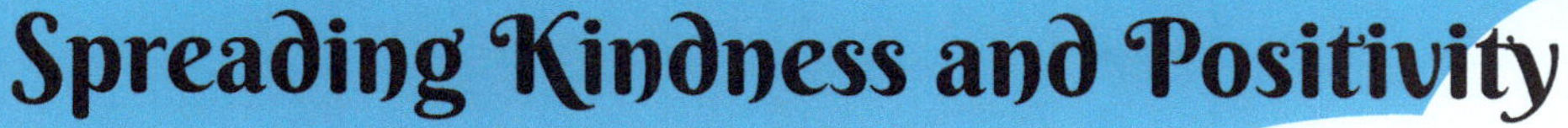

Spreading Kindness and Positivity

Sarah and Zakaria embraced the teachings of Islam by spreading kindness and positivity in their interactions, both with each other and with those around them. They aimed to uplift others, inspiring peace and harmony within their social circles.

Seeking Inner Peace

Sarah and Zakaria focused on seeking inner peace through their faith. They engaged in acts of worship, seeking knowledge, practicing mindfulness, and reflecting on the beauty of the Quranic verses, finding solace and tranquility in their connection with Allah (SWT).

Strengthening the Community

Sarah and Zakaria recognized their role in
strengthening the community through service
and activities that promoted unity and peace.
They actively participated in charitable
activities, volunteering and promoting unity
among their peers, thereby fostering
an environment of peace and harmony.

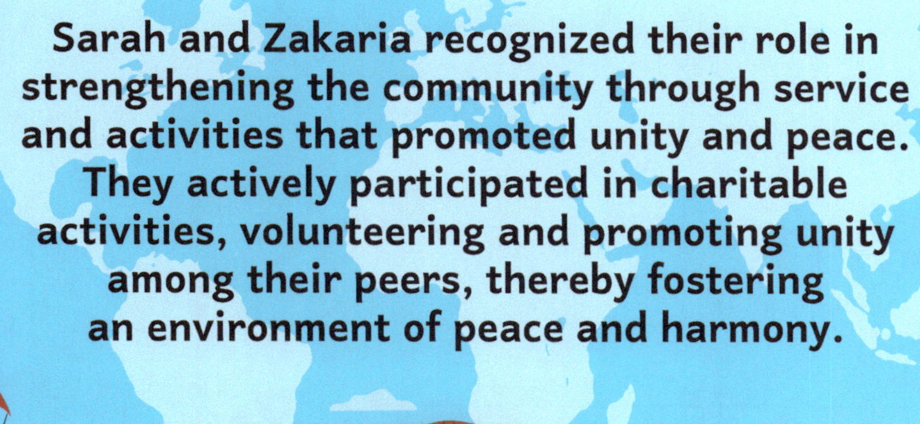

Continual Self-Evaluation

Sarah and Zakaria understood the importance of continual self-evaluation. They regularly assessed their actions and intentions and the impact these had on their personal and social lives, seeking to align themselves with the teachings of Islam. They recognized that true friendship allows for personal development while maintaining a sense of harmony and peace.

Seeking Blessings in Friendships

Sarah and Zakaria sought to find blessings (barakah) in their friendship. They recognized that a friendship rooted in faith would bring them such blessings by finding tranquility and a sense of purpose in their personal and social lives.

Striving for Excellence

Sarah and Zakaria strove for excellence in all aspects of their lives. They aimed to excel academically, spiritually, and morally, recognizing that their friendship should contribute positively to their pursuit of a peaceful and fulfilling life.

The Importance of Patience

Sarah and Zakaria faced conflicts and disagreements like any other friends, but they practiced patience in their friendship.
They understood that building a lasting bond takes time and effort, and they were willing to invest in their relationship in order to reap the rewards of sustainable peace and happiness.
In the Holy Quran,
Allah (SWT) advises us:

"And obey Allah and His Messenger, and do not dispute and [thus] lose courage and [then] your strength would depart; and be patient. Indeed,
Allah is with the patient"
(Surah Al-Anfal, 8:46).

This verse highlights the importance of obedience to Allah and His Messenger. Developing a close friendship with Allah involves following His guidance and having patience when facing challenges and difficulties.

Holding onto Faith

Sarah and Zakaria held onto their faith and consistently sought Allah's guidance in their friendship.
They relied on the strength and wisdom that came from their Islamic beliefs, finding solace and direction in moments of confusion or uncertainty,
knowing that Allah (SWT) was the ultimate source of wisdom and guidance.
In the Holy Quran, Allah (SWT) says,

"Indeed, [O Muhammad],
you do not guide whom you like,
but Allah guides whom He wills.
And He is most knowing of the [rightly] guided"
(Surah Al-Qasas, 28:56).

This verse reminds us that ultimately, it is Allah who guides individuals. Even if we have good intentions to guide others, it is up to Allah to open their hearts to guidance.
Therefore, it is important to focus on our own relationship with Allah and surround ourselves with positive influences,
rather than trying to change the hearts of those who indulge in bad company.

Reflecting on the Journey

Sarah and Zakaria reflected on their journey together, recognizing the growth and transformation they had experienced. They also shared their ideal moments and how to inspire their peers to build friendships rooted in faith and peace.
They shared their experiences, challenges, and the lessons they learned from the Quran and Al Hadith, spreading awareness and understanding. They were grateful for the lessons learned and for the peace they found in their friendship.

A Lasting Friendship

Sarah and Zakaria concluded their journey with a lasting friendship that brought them peace and joy. They continued to support and encourage each other on their paths to becoming righteous individuals, guided by the teachings of the Holy Quran and the traditions of the Prophet Muhammad (peace be upon him). They vowed to use their friendship to promote peace and harmony in their personal and social lives, knowing that true fulfillment lies in building friendships according to the teachings of Islam.

Finally, these teachings are not only for Sarah and Zakaria; everyone can find key insights from the Holy Quran and the role model of the Prophet Muhammad (SAW) regarding friendships and flirtationships. In this, the importance of nurturing positive friendships and adhering to Islamic principles to maintain a healthy balance in people's lives cannot be over-stated.

www.ingramcontent.com/pod-product-compliance
Lightning Source LLC
Chambersburg PA
CBHW042157030726
47599CB00004B/769